CONSERVING RAINFORESTS

Martin Banks

Acid Rain
Conserving the Atmosphere
Conserving the Polar Regions
Farming and the Environment
Protecting the Oceans
Protecting Wildlife
The Spread of Deserts
Waste and Recycling

Cover: An area of rainforest in the
Genting Highlands of Malaysia.

Series editor: Sue Hadden
Series designer: Ross George

First published in 1989 by
Wayland (Publishers) Ltd
61 Western Road, Hove
East Sussex BN3 1JD, England

© Copyright 1989 Wayland (Publishers) Ltd

This edition published in 1991 by
Wayland (Publishers) Ltd

British Library Cataloguing in Publication Data
Banks, Martin, 1947-
    Conserving rainforests
    1. Tropical rainforests. Conservation.
    I. Title   II. Series
    333.75

HARDBACK ISBN 1-85210-695-6

PAPERBACK ISBN 0-7502-0272-6

Typeset by Lizzie George, Wayland.
Printed in Italy by G. Canale C.S.p.A., Turin

Contents

Some years ago I was part of a group visiting the hills of south-west India to search for a rare species of monkey which lives in the tropical rainforest there. As we entered the forest, the sunlight faded because it was filtered through the dense foliage. We found ourselves in an area dominated by enormous small-leaved evergreen trees, their trunks festooned with creepers and vines. Beneath them grew a layer of shrubs and ferns, among which darted brightly-coloured butterflies and birds such as flycatchers.

We were hoping to see the wanderoo, a rare South-east Asian macaque. We spent hours slowly walking through the dense forest, peering into the dimly-lit upper branches of the trees, where we knew the monkeys could be found. Finally we located some and were able to watch them at close quarters as they fed and moved through the trees. The troop of monkeys was large and contained many young. They would be safe for the future, we thought, as this forest was part of a protected wildlife sanctuary.

Rainforests are among the richest habitats in the world. They contain an incredible diversity of animal life, including many tree-dwelling mammals like this squirrel monkey from South America.

Some rainforests have already been completely destroyed, along with all their animal life.

Eventually the troop of monkeys moved out of sight and we walked on to the edge of the forest. We emerged in brilliant sunshine to a scene of utter devastation. As far as the eye could see in any direction, the ground was bare of trees, covered in the roots and stumps of those that had been felled. Enormous stacks of timber were piled high, awaiting transportation. A few tall isolated trees still stood overlooking the destruction all around them.

Not so long ago, the whole area before us had no doubt been covered in rainforest. The lower slopes of the hillsides had been the first to be cleared to create tea plantations. Now the higher forests were being cleared, too, leaving only small pockets of rainforest. Later we discovered that, despite being a wildlife sanctuary, the rainforest we had visited covered an area of less than one square kilometre. We were left to wonder sadly how long the monkeys, and all the other plants and animals we had seen, could continue to survive in their little patch of rainforest.

The account you have just read concerned the Indian rainforest, but very similar stories could be told about rainforest areas of Africa, South America and South-east Asia. All the world's rainforests are under great threat of destruction and their future survival is in doubt. This book will explain why the rainforests are in such danger and what can be done to save them before it is too late.

There are many different sorts of rainforests. This photograph shows the astounding variety of trees that grow in the Equatorial rainforests. The photograph was taken in Ecuador, a country which was named after the Equator.

What is a rainforest?

Rainforests are one of the richest and most diverse habitats which still exist in the world today. They are found at both temperate and tropical latitudes of the earth, but tropical rainforest, which is found closer to the Equator, contains the most plant and animal life.

The earliest record we have that describes the appearance and atmosphere of a rainforest is that of the explorer, Christopher Columbus. In his voyages of discovery around the world, he opened up new trade and shipping routes. Columbus is best remembered for his journey to the Americas, but he was also the first European to locate the West Indies. In 1492 Columbus landed on the mountainous island of Haiti. Entering its rainforest, he beautifully described the sights and sounds that greeted him:

'I never beheld so fair a thing; trees beautiful and green and different from ours, with flowers and fruits each according to their kind, many and little birds which sing very sweetly.'

Four centuries after Columbus' arrival, a German botanist gave these forests their modern name 'rainforest'. The many travellers and scientists who had visited them in between referred to them simply as forests or tropical forests. While many of them marvelled at the abundance of animals and plants they contained, it is only more recently that we have begun to realize just how exceptional and unique a rainforest really is.

What exactly is a tropical rainforest, and how does it differ from other forests? There are many different sorts of rainforests. Some botanists recognize thirty or more, including evergreen forests, semi-deciduous forests, cloud forests at high altitudes on mountains and lowland forests which grow along the banks of rivers. We can distinguish two main types. Firstly, Equatorial rainforests grow close to the Equator and experience very high temperatures and rainfall. The trees in these forests are mainly evergreens, and there is little variation in the seasons of the year. Secondly, further away from the Equator, lower temperatures and rainfall combine with more variable seasons to produce a different rainforest type. The forests here are termed 'moist' or 'semi-deciduous'. They do not have quite the same abundance of plants and animals as Equatorial rainforests.

Many people assume that a rainforest is what is popularly referred to as a jungle. To most of us, the word jungle conjures up the image of a very dense growth of tall grass, shrubs and trees, full of trailing creepers and an assortment of noisy and dangerous animals. Jungles are thought of as impenetrable to all but the most intrepid explorer, armed with a sharp machete.

In fact, a tropical rainforest bears little relation to our notions of the jungle. It has clearly defined layers of vegetation. The crowns of the tall rainforest trees form a dense, leafy layer called the canopy. At a much lower level grow bushes and shrubs which form what is called the understorey. In Equatorial rainforests, the dense canopy excludes all but a few shafts of sunlight so the understorey contains relatively little vegetation, while the forest floor consists of bare earth carpeted with leaves and rotting vegetation.

Rainforests can be found from high altitudes right down to sea level, as here in Surinam.

The understorey of this Javan rainforest is a thick tangle of vines and creepers.

Beneath the trees in the rainforest it is quiet and dim. Though animals are abundant, they are seldom seen or heard. Strange bird calls disturb the still air occasionally, while a crashing of branches high up in the treetops gives away the presence of a troop of monkeys or a giant squirrel. A flock of gaily coloured parrots, or a group of brightly patterned butterflies bring sudden life to a quiet sunlit clearing. But the atmosphere of the rainforest is really more like that of a dimly-lit cathedral than a jungle.

Where are the rainforests?

Tropical rainforest is the natural vegetation of the lands which lie along the Equator, between the Tropics of Cancer to the North and Capricorn to the South. The main requirements for the growth of rainforest are a heavy annual rainfall, normally between 400 mm and 1,000 mm a year, together with a high average temperature of around 27 °C. Further away from the Equator, rainfall of over 100 mm per year and fluctuating temperatures produce the semi-deciduous type of forest.

Rainforests of the World

Central America

South America

Many millions of years ago, when the climate of the earth was much warmer, rainforests extended across much of the world, far to the north and south of their current distribution. Pollen grains of rainforest plants have been discovered in places as far north as London and

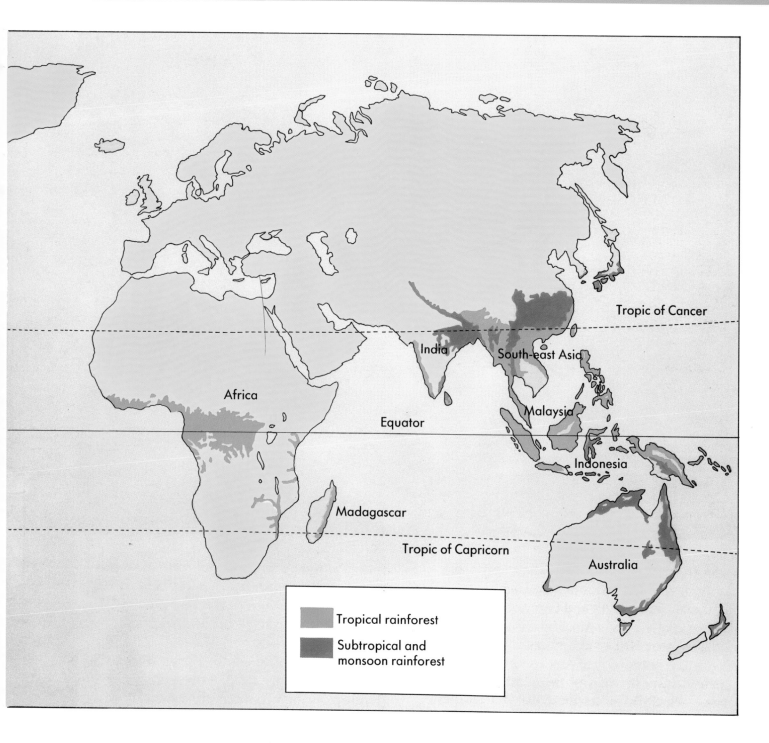

even in Alaska. So rainforest represents one of the most ancient, or primeval, natural habitats of the world. Just a few thousand years ago, 14 per cent of the earth's land surface was covered by rainforest of one type or another. Within the last two hundred years, over half that area has been converted into pasture, farmland or simply wasteland.

Today rainforest is only found in South and Central America, central Africa and the island of Madagascar in the Indian Ocean, and in South-east Asia. The Asian forests are found from

India through Malaysia and the Philippines to northern Australia. The largest areas of existing rainforest are in South and Central America. The vast basin of the River Amazon and its tributaries, contains over half of the rainforests left in the world. The rainforests of Amazonia represent the greatest unspoilt areas of tropical rainforest left in the world today, and harbour an enormous wealth of plant and animal life. Brazil alone contains a third of the remaining rainforests. Also in Brazil, there are the last small remnants of a once extensive rainforest which stretched along the Atlantic coast. This area contains some of the rarest species of monkeys left in the world.

Across the Atlantic Ocean, the rainforests of the Congo basin in central Africa have a similar

The largest remaining areas of rainforests are in South and Central America, particularly in the Amazon basin and in Brazil, which has a third of all rainforest left in the world.

appearance to those of the New World. The animals and plants here, however, are quite different from their counterparts which live in the forests of the New World. The forests of Madagascar, which split off from the mainland of Africa millions of years ago, contain a quite different assortment of flora and fauna from the rainforests of central Africa.

Rainforests are also found in a number of different countries in South-east Asia, from the north-eastern tip of Australia to southern China.

Thousands of islands, large and small, make up the country collectively called Indonesia. The larger islands of Borneo, Sumatra, Java and New Guinea all have rainforests too. All together, South-east Asia contains about a quarter of the world's remaining rainforests.

Each of the three main rainforest areas are separated from one another by thousands of kilometres of ocean and they each contain their own unique plants and animals. The forests have not always been isolated in this way. Originally, the land masses on which they are found were joined together. When the continents split apart long ago, most of the flora and fauna of each developed differently. However, a few species of rainforest plants and animals inhabit more than one of the main areas, and a handful actually occur in all three. This is evidence of the fact that all the rainforests originally lay within a continuous land mass.

Diagram 1 shows the earth's continents joined together in one land mass, called Pangaea. It is thought that there was little variation in the plant and animal life that inhabited the rainforests of Pangaea.

About 180 million years ago, the land mass of Pangaea began to break up. Eventually, the continents reached the positions we know today, as shown in diagram 2. With the continents now separated, plant and animal life evolved differently in each one. This explains the variation found today in the wildlife of the world's rainforests.

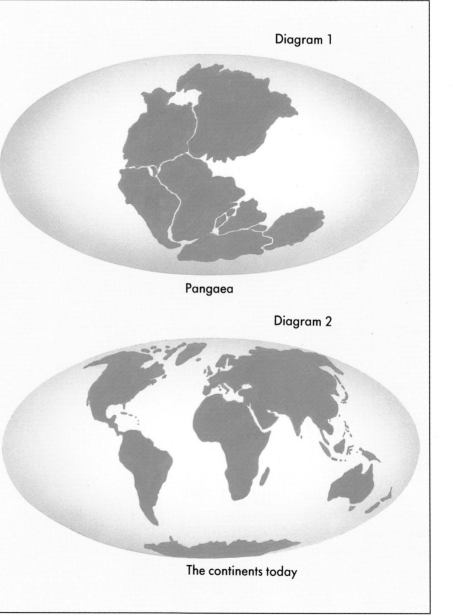

Diagram 1

Pangaea

Diagram 2

The continents today

The structure of a rainforest

As we have read, a tropical rainforest consists of several distinct layers. The explorer Alexander von Humboldt called it 'a forest above a forest'. Each of these layers creates a separate habitat for the animals and plants which live there. So a rainforest actually supports several quite different plant and animal communities.

The top layer of the rainforest is created by the canopy. The tall trees mostly reach a height of between 30 m and 60 m. Their trunks are normally smooth for most of this height, only branching out to form the crown at the limit of their growth. The crown of each tree almost touches the next, forming a mass of leaves and branches which prevents the sunlight from reaching the lower layers. A few trees grow much higher than others, pushing up through the level of the canopy. These giants of the forest, with their crowns standing high above the rest, are called emergents.

The second layer of the rainforest is often called the understorey. It consists of shrubs, ferns and small trees which are able to thrive in the dimly-lit dampness below the canopy. Ferns and palms have long thin leaves to help them absorb the little sunlight that filters down from the canopy. In rainforests near the Equator, many of the trees are evergreen and so form a canopy that blots out the sun throughout the year. The

The diagram below illustrates the vegetation layers typically found in rainforests. The vegetation of the understorey is very sparse in Equatorial rainforests.

emergent layer

canopy

understorey

lianas

forest floor

understorey of these forests is very sparse.

The forest floor forms the lowest layer of the rainforest. The ground is carpeted with a shallow layer of leaf litter. This is produced from the leaves that fall from the trees throughout the year. The leaf litter is broken down by many insects that feed on it and it also decomposes quickly in the humid atmosphere. The thin layer that remains on the ground provides ideal growing conditions for all kinds of fungi. Some are shaped like parasols, some like glass threads and some are even luminous.

Left *The dark, damp conditions due to lack of sunlight encourage the growth of many types of fungi like these South American ones.*

Below *The crowns of the trees in the canopy grow close together, sometimes broken by an emergent tree.*

Adaptations of rainforest trees

Rainforest trees look and behave quite differently from most other trees of the world. Unlike trees that grow in the temperate or subarctic zones, those of rainforests are not exposed to seasonal changes. Therefore they may flower, produce fruit or seeds, and shed leaves at any time of year. Rainforest trees are called broadleaved evergreens. Their leaves are specially designed to repel rainwater, which falls on them at regular intervals. They have a waxy covering and a pointed 'drip tip' which allows rainwater and fallen seeds to run off, so keeping the leaves clean and dry.

The vast trees of rainforests use various means to support their immense weight. Some, like palms, have stilt roots growing down from their trunk or branches. Many of the largest trees have solid buttress roots growing from their bases to give them a broader-based support.

Every so often a giant forest tree falls down, creating a large gap in the canopy, through which sunlight can reach the forest floor. This encourages the sudden growth of seeds lying dormant in the leaf litter. Soon a number of seedlings will be rapidly growing. In time, the fastest-growing one or two will fill the gap in the canopy and blot out the sunlight once more.

A beautiful rainforest orchid.

Rainforest plants

Rainforests contain many interesting plants. Climbers, like lianas grow like thick rope between the trees. Mosses and lichens grow on the trunks and branches of the trees, thriving in the moist atmosphere. Some other plants, such as orchids and bromeliads, grow out of the bark. They are called epiphytes, which means that they grow on another plant and obtain all their nutrients from the water and dead plant matter that falls on them from the canopy.

Growing rainforest plants

Some rainforest plants have become popular house plants. These include bromeliads of various kinds and foliage plants such as weeping figs, Ficus benjamina. Many of the palms, hibiscus and orchids sold as houseplants also originated in rainforests.

You can try to grow your own rainforest plants, such as oranges, lemons and grapefruit. Simply plant a pip in some potting compost, adding a little water. Keep the pot in a warm place out of bright light, and water it occasionally. After a while, the pip should germinate. Your plant may not bear fruit but it will produce lovely scented flowers.

Opposite *Rainforest trees are enormous compared with most other trees of the world. The photograph shows a giant tree growing in south-east Madagascar. Even its buttress roots far exceed the height of this man.*

Above *The enormous Victoria regia waterlily grows on the Amazon. Its large leaves can support a child's weight.*

Below *Rafflesia arnoldii is the largest flower in the world, measuring up to a metre across. Its enormous flowers smell of rotting flesh, which attracts flies to pollinate it. It is found in tropical rainforests in Indonesia where its future, like the rainforest's, is uncertain.*

No two rainforests are exactly alike in the number and variety of species they contain. Those of South America tend to be richer in plants than the forests of central Africa, while the South-east Asian forests contain the greatest diversity of animal life. However, the basic pattern of layers is common to all rainforests, wherever they are. Moreover, the total number and variety of plants contained in rainforests is far greater than anywhere else. The forests of Panama in Central America have more plant species than are found in the whole of Europe. Although there are so many species, individual species are often found only in relatively small areas and in small numbers. This makes them particularly vulnerable when forests are extensively cut down.

Left *Tarsiers are nocturnal creatures of the Indonesian rainforests. They mainly feed on insects, such as this cicada.*

Right *Tapirs are smaller relatives of rhinoceroses. They are found in the rainforests of both South America and South–east Asia. The photograph shows the endangered Malaysian tapir.*

The secondary layer of the forest also has its own mammal inhabitants. There are various small climbing species such as the American possums, Australian opossums and the African bushbabies. They spend much of the day asleep, usually inside hollows in the trunks of trees. After dark they emerge to feed on insects.

The bareness of the forest floor discourages many larger mammals from living there. Small rodents like mice and agoutis of South America make their homes in the shelter of hollow logs and under shrubs. In Africa tiny antelopes called duikers nibble the fallen leaves of the forest floor. Larger mammals tend to be solitary like the

okapi, a very secretive and smaller relative of the giraffe, which inhabits the rainforests of central Africa. The Amazon forests and those of South-east Asia both contain tapirs, which are smaller relatives of the rhinoceroses. They are one of the species which provides evidence of the original land link between all the rainforests. Several species of cats inhabit rainforests. Best known are the jaguar, margay and ocelot, which range from Central to South America, and the leopard cats of South-east Asia. All of these cats are accomplished tree-climbers, although they spend most of the time on the ground.

The margay of South America is endangered through habitat loss and hunting.

Above Humming-birds feed on the nectar of rainforest flowers and help to pollinate them.

Over half the mammals which live in rainforests are found high up in the canopy. This is also the home of many species of birds, which are attracted by the abundance of fruits and seeds. When a forest tree is fruiting, it is visited not only by monkeys, fruit bats and squirrels, but also parrots and hornbills or toucans. The parrot family is an extensive one and its largest and most brightly coloured members, called macaws, live in the South American rainforests. Macaws have

Right Toucans live in the South American rainforests, feeding on fruits and berries.

very strong beaks for cracking open fruits and nuts. A flock of macaws provides a brilliant spectacle as it flies, screeching loudly, through a forest clearing. Toucans are another family of fruit-eating birds. They have enormous, boldly patterned beaks which they use to pluck fruits and berries from the trees. In the forests of South-east Asia, hornbills live in a way similar to that of toucans in South America. Their heavy, flapping flight over the treetops is a familiar sight in almost any Asian rainforest.

The large fruit-eating birds, like parrots, toucans and hornbills, all play an important role in maintaining the rainforest. Like some monkeys, they help to spread the seeds of the trees on which they feed. The birds swallow the fruits whole and then fly some distance before passing out the undigested seeds in their droppings.

Some birds help to maintain the forest in a different way, pollinating the forest trees by feeding on the nectar produced by their flowers. The tiny jewel-like humming-birds of South America, and the sunbirds of Asia and Africa are all equipped with long, thin bills and tongues with which they sip nectar from flowers. Humming-birds in particular have very rapid wingbeats which help them hover while they feed. In South America, humming-birds are found not only in the hot, humid lowland forests, but also in cloud forests at high altitudes in the mountains.

The lower storeys of the rainforest contain some of the most brilliantly-coloured birds on earth. The forests of New Guinea are the home of several species of birds of paradise. The males assemble together at clearings in the forest where they dance and show off their beautiful plumage, in order to attract the dull-coloured females. South American cock-of-the-rocks, with their brilliant orange or scarlet plumage, are the New World counterparts of the birds of paradise.

Other birds live on the forest floor itself. The Asian forests are home to colourful peacocks and

Birds of paradise are among the most spectacular rainforest birds.

pheasants, and the jungle fowl, which is the ancestor of our farmyard hens. The South American rainforests contain large turkey-like birds called curassows.

Because so many rainforest species live in the canopy, the hunting animals of the forest concentrate their attention there too. One of the most powerful hunters in the rainforest is an enormous eagle. Three different species occur, one in each of the three main rainforest areas. The monkey-eating eagle is found in South-east Asia, the crowned eagle in Africa, and the harpy eagle in South America. All of them are very similar, swooping down into the canopy to grab birds, squirrels and even monkeys in their immensely powerful talons. These eagles are the largest and most powerful predators of the rainforest canopy. They rear their young in nests in the huge emergent trees of the rainforest.

Tropical rainforests undoubtedly contain more species of birds than any other habitat. A typical small patch of rainforest may contain 400 species, far more than a complete country like the British Isles. In fact, the rainforests of Amazonia contain a fifth of all the bird species found in the world.

More unusual creatures

Birds and mammals are the largest and best-known rainforest animals, but rainforests also contain a vast array of other creatures. These include reptiles and amphibians and so many different species of invertebrates, that it is quite impossible to count them. All these smaller inhabitants occupy their own special areas in the forest, just like the mammals and birds.

Many of the snakes and lizards found in the rainforest are excellent climbers. Some of the snakes live high up in the canopy, climbing along branches and hiding among the leaves whose colours they closely resemble. Contrary to popular imagination, most of them are small and thin. Living and hunting as they do high up in the trees, they would be at a distinct disadvantage if they were too large and heavy.

Right *In the rainforest of Java, Indonesia, a flying lizard glides in mid-air. Its body flaps are spread to form 'wings'.*

Below *The kingsnake lives on the ground. Its colouring mimics that of a poisonous species, the coral snake, as a way of avoiding predators.*

Some of the reptiles and amphibians which live in the forest canopy have developed special techniques for travelling from tree to tree. In South-east Asia there are snakes, lizards and frogs which 'fly' using the same technique as the flying squirrels. Flying frogs have very large webbed toes which act like tiny parachutes when the frog jumps into the air. Flying lizards have flaps of skin on the sides of their bodies, which they can raise like sails to carry them through the air from one branch to another. Possibly the strangest aerial traveller of all is the flying snake. By flattening its body and coiling into an 'S' shape, the snake can catch more air and glide downhill from one tree trunk to the next.

The warm, moist conditions of the rainforest

Frogs are found at almost every level in the rainforest. Many of them are specially adapted to live in trees. This red-eyed tree frog of Costa Rica lays its eggs on leaves.

are perfect for the development of amphibians, like frogs and salamanders. Many of these creatures live in the rotting vegetation on the forest floor. But a number of frogs live in the trees, rather than on the ground. Some of these frogs have most unusual breeding cycles. They lay their eggs on leaves, and when the tadpoles hatch, the parent frogs carry them on their backs to the tiny pools of water contained in the leaves of bromeliad plants. Here each tadpole has its own nursery where it will grow to full size.

So far we have looked at the astonishing variety of plants and animals that live in rainforests. We should not forget that people have also lived in them for thousands of years, successfully using the forest materials to build their homes and the plants as food and medicines.

Today about 200 million people live in rainforests. The South American rainforest is inhabited by various tribes of Amerindians, or American Indians. Pygmies and Bushmen live in

The ancestors of these Pygmies have been living in the rainforest of central Africa for thousands of years, using local materials to build their homes and forest plants for food and medicines. Now their unique lifestyle is threatened as the rainforest is opened up.

some parts of the African rainforests. Many different peoples live in the South-east Asian rainforest, including Pygmies in parts of the

Philippines, the Biami and Gibusi peoples of New Guinea, and the Sianh Daya in Borneo.

Each particular rainforest tribe has its own special traditions and beliefs, although all the original people's way of life is broadly similar. Traditionally rainforest peoples hunted wild animals and gathered seeds for food. Today many of them clear small patches of forest in which they grow food crops, such as maize, cassava and sweet potatoes. Rainforest peoples have a special knowledge of the native forest plants, which they use as effective medicines to treat many ailments.

The unique way of life of rainforest peoples survived unchanged for thousands of years. It was first threatened when Europeans arrived in South America in the early sixteenth century and disturbed the peoples living in remote forest areas. At that time the number of Amerindians was about four million. Today their numbers have been reduced to fewer than 100,000. The numbers of African and Asian rainforest peoples have also declined over the centuries.

The Amerindians of South America flourished in the vast rainforests of the Amazon basin, until the arrival of Europeans in the early part of the sixteenth century. Today tribes still survive in remote rainforest areas. These Nahva Indians of Peru were first contacted by 'outsiders' in 1986.

Left Original peoples who inhabit rainforest regions are skilled at building homes from forest materials. This rainforest village is in New Guinea.

Below Whole tribes of rainforest-dwellers have lost their ancestral homes and been forced to adopt new cultures. The new housing developments are a bleak alternative to traditional rainforest homes.

The price of 'progress'

The rapid expansion of modern technology has particularly endangered rainforest peoples. When new roads are built through rainforests, once-remote areas become immediately accessible. Therefore it is easier to clear the trees to create land for farming or to build new settlements. Whole tribes of rainforest peoples

have been driven away from their homes when outsiders arrive to clear and develop their patch of forest. Those who remain are forced to adapt to a very different way of life. For the first time they encounter different people bringing new religions and values, different methods of education, modern technology, new foods and alcohol. They are exposed to different diseases, against which they have no natural immunity.

Many tribes have become extinct as a result of contact with other civilizations. Eighty-seven groups of Amerindians formerly living in the Brazilian rainforest have been exterminated this century. In Indonesia millions of forest-dwelling peoples are being relocated far away from their

How long will these Huli tribesmen in Papua New Guinea be able to practise their traditions?

homes in a government-sponsored project. Enormous numbers of them have been moved from the overcrowded islands of Bali, Java and Madura to Irian Jaya, the Indonesian half of New Guinea. There they must adopt a completely different lifestyle.

In this chapter we have seen how the opening up of remote rainforest areas affects the traditional peoples living in them. In the next chapter we shall learn why rainforests are being destroyed so rapidly, and what other far-reaching consequences this may have.

The disappearing rainforests

There is no doubt that rainforests form the richest and most diverse habitat on earth. Yet rainforests are also suffering the most from the destructive influences of humankind. The world's rainforests are being cleared at an alarming rate. Every year

'At the present rate of destruction, all accessible tropical rainforests will have disappeared by the end of this century.'

Report of the United Nations

Estimated area of rainforest by the year 2000

	1950	1975	2000
1000			
750			
500			
250			

area in millions of hectares

4-5 million hectares are completely destroyed. This means that 12-20 hectares disappear somewhere in the world every minute of every day. In addition, one animal species becomes extinct every half an hour.

All of the main rainforests are under similar attack. Until recently, Africa was losing its forests at the rate of 2 million hectares a year, while in South-east Asia, the remaining forests are disappearing at only a slightly slower rate. Central America now has only a third of the forests it used to contain thirty years ago.

Why are rainforests vanishing at such a tremendous rate? The answer lies in the needs of people, who cut down the forests in the belief that to do so will provide them with immediate benefits. In tropical countries where rainforests occur, most of the population outside towns and cities is engaged in small-scale farming. For these people, the forests have no obvious value, but cutting them down and clearing them away makes valuable farmland available. At the same time, the timber provides much-needed income

This South American saw mill provides employment for local people, but does cutting down the forest make good economic sense?

for most countries that possess rainforests. Some species of hardwood trees found in rainforests have a high commercial value. Teak and mahogany have fine, durable wood much in demand in the western world for the manufacture of many products including furniture and boats. The less valuable trees can all be converted into pulp, plywood and paper.

A procession of logging trucks in Malaysia.

Modern machinery can cut down the forests at an alarming rate. Rainforests are disappearing wherever they stand in the way of progress.

Left *Rainforests are also destroyed so that the ground can be mined for precious metals. Here manganese is being mined in Brazil.*

Nowadays, modern technology allows the forests to be cut down more rapidly than ever. Heavy plant and machinery like bulldozers and cranes can clear large tracts of forest in a fraction of the time it used to take men using axes. There are more reasons for removing the forests, in addition to timber. Roads, dams, irrigation channels, canals, pipe and power lines are all increasingly needed in the developing countries. The forests which stand in their way are an inconvenient obstacle in the march of progress. Today, in a matter of a few months or a year, a large tract of rainforest can be converted into an enormous plantation or cattle ranch. It is grazing land for cattle which has replaced so much rainforest in Latin America, where beef farming is one of the main sources of revenue.

The consequences of deforestation

It may seem sad but understandable that rainforests are destroyed to make way for the necessary growth and expansion in developing countries. Unfortunately, when the forests are cut down, they do not always provide suitable land for their new purpose. Rainforest soils are very old, and have supported countless generations of plant growth. They are poor in nutrients, which means that crops grown on them cannot prosper in the same way as the specially-adapted native plants of the rainforest. When the forests are converted into farmland, they remain fertile for only a few years. Then more forest has to be cleared and the process repeated. The peoples who live in the forests know this, and employ a 'slash and burn' method of agriculture, clearing a small patch of forest for temporary cultivation before moving on again. Now, however, this is happening on a gigantic scale, leaving vast areas of barren wasteland where crops and even grass fail to grow.

Above *The lifeless reality of an area of rainforest that has been burned down.*

Left *'Slash and burn' agriculture in a west African forest. This practice results in extensive areas being cleared, even though the land can only be used to grow crops for a very short time.*

Deforestation and erosion

Where rainforests have been cleared, erosion often occurs. Without the tree cover, rain cannot be absorbed and so it drains off the ground, gradually washing away the topsoil. Stripped of its nutrients, the remaining soil is of little value for crop-growing. The soil that has been washed away causes rivers to become blocked with silt. When tropical rainstorms occur, the blocked rivers burst their banks, causing extensive flooding. Such floods have already occurred in South America and South-east Asia.

deforested area

silting up

flooding

Removing the forest cover can have very serious side effects, too. Rainforests are directly responsible for local rainfall, since the giant trees absorb a great deal of rainfall, which they slowly release as additional moisture into the atmosphere. Cutting down the forests will reduce the rainfall of the region, eventually to the extent that desert conditions prevail. Stripped of its network of plant cover, the land is more prone to erosion. In turn, the soil eroded from the land can silt up rivers and lead to flooding. In India, severe flooding takes place annually in the river deltas, as a result of deforestation high in the Himalayan mountains. Forty years ago, almost half of Ethiopia was covered in forest, which provided vital water for crop irrigation. Today, only five per cent of Ethiopia's forests remain. As a result of this, Ethiopia's enormous human population is victim of famine, drought and floods.

Soil erosion takes place as a direct result of cutting down the forests. These eroded hills are in Java, Indonesia.

On a world-wide scale too, the consequences of rainforest destruction are far-reaching. Rainforests are known to regulate global weather patterns. In tropical regions, over a billion people depend on the water generated by tropical forests to irrigate their crops. Even in the northern hemisphere, destruction of rainfall cycles and the build-up of carbon dioxide in the earth's atmosphere are the likely results of large scale tropical deforestation. Eventually this could lead to a general warming of the atmosphere called the 'greenhouse effect' which itself could result in increased melting of the polar icecaps and subsequent rises in sea level.

Soil erosion causes landslides, silting-up of rivers and flooding, resulting in crop failures and national disasters.

Rainfall and rainforests

Rainforests play a major role in regulating climatic conditions, especially rainfall. The huge trees draw up a great deal of water with their roots. Later the water is released as a vapour through the leaves in the process called transpiration. The evaporated water condenses into clouds in the atmosphere, to fall again as rain.
When large areas of rainforest are destroyed, the local water cycle is affected. Without the rainforests to store the water, serious droughts occur more frequently.

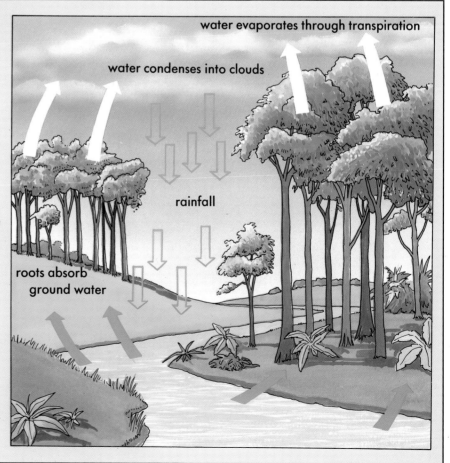

water evaporates through transpiration

water condenses into clouds

rainfall

roots absorb ground water

Once a rainforest has been destroyed, it cannot be replaced. Even if only the larger trees are removed, the fragile ecosystem will be destroyed. In the process, a unique community of plants and animals will be lost forever. Many of them are of immeasurable value to people. For centuries, people who live in the rainforests have used the chemical compounds of many plant species as drugs and medicines. Now the value of these herbal remedies has been recognized by modern science too. Curare, ipecac, wild yam and Madagascar periwinkle are just a few examples of plants whose compounds are used to fight major diseases such as cancer, leukaemia, muscular and heart diseases. They also form the basic ingredients of birth control hormones, stimulants and tranquillizing drugs. Possibly the best known drug which originates from a rainforest plant is quinine. Quinine comes from the bark of a South American tree, the Cinchona or 'Fever Bark' tree. It has proved to be a very effective cure for malaria.

Rainforest plants are equally vital to agriculture and industry. Tea, coffee, bananas, oranges, lemons, peanuts, pineapples and guavas are all native rainforest plants. Over half

Local peoples have always used plants as medicines. Now science has discovered the value of rainforest plants.

Many fruits and cereals which form part of our staple diet are derived from rainforest plants. The South American passion flower is a popular plant in gardens today, while the fruit is widely imported for culinary use.

the cereals eaten by humans, including rice and maize, originated in the rainforest. Industry, too, has already benefited greatly from rainforest products. Most famous is the rubber industry, dependent on a tree which grows wild in the rainforests of South America and South-east Asia. Other industrial products such as resins for paints, oils, waxes, soaps and plastics have also been produced from rainforest plants. Undoubtedly other materials having similar valuable properties remain to be discovered, but only providing there are still rainforests left in which to find them.

Today 40 per cent of the world's rainforests have already vanished. The remaining forests are still being cut down at such a rate that some countries will have lost all their forests by the year 2000. However, before it is too late, efforts are being made to halt this drastic loss and conserve at least some of the forests in an unspoilt state.

Rubber is an important rainforest product. In the photograph a Brazilian woman collects latex from a tree.

How can we halt the destruction?

Most rainforests are found in the developing countries – the economically poorer countries. It is very easy for the richer, Western nations to criticize them for destroying rainforests. However, in the process of 'civilization' the more advanced industrial nations of the West have also sacrificed much of their own natural heritage. Today they continue to destroy and pollute the world's natural resources. Therefore they have certainly not set a good example for the developing countries to follow.

The Western world must share with the developing countries the responsibility of trying to conserve the remaining rainforests before it is too late. The Western nations can offer great expertise in biology, agriculture, forestry and other fields that are relevant to the situation facing our rainforests today.

How can we stop the destruction of tropical rainforests? It is difficult, but there are several possible ways in which the felling of these magnificent forests might be brought under reasonable control. If current methods of agriculture were changed, this would reduce the continual need for land and, therefore, slow down the rate at which the forests are felled. Because the soils of rainforests are ancient and, therefore, poor in nutrients, they cannot sustain annual cereal crops successfully, However, some crops can be beneficial to rainforest soils, for example various types of palms. These trees thrive naturally on the soils in the understorey of the forest. As they grow into mature trees, palms help to stabilize the soil. So erosion is prevented while palm nut oil provides a useful source of income. This is not a simple answer for every area of rainforest in the world. However, it demonstrates that it is possible to grow profitable crops without using the shifting method of agriculture which is so disastrous for the forests.

Right *Palm trees thrive naturally in the rainforest understorey. Where forests have been cut down, oil palms can be grown. They produce palm nut oil and they help to stabilize the unprotected soil.*

Selective logging means that only some trees, not the whole forest, are cut down. Gradually the forest will regenerate, just as it does when a huge tree naturally crashes down. The photograph was taken in Victoria Falls rainforest, Zimbabwe.

Another threat to rainforests that must be resolved is timber felling. Clear cut felling, in which all the large trees of the forest are cut down, certainly means the end of the forest. Selective logging is a less harmful alternative, in which timber can be harvested without destroying entire forests. Here only certain trees are removed at one time. Over the years new tall trees grow and fill the gaps, just as they do when a gap in the forest canopy is created naturally.

The timber industry causes further problems. It entails the creation of roads and tracks into the forest, so that the timber can be transported. The dragging away of tree trunks also harms the forest. If such damage could be avoided, and if selective logging were widely introduced, the prospects of rainforests would be brighter.

Ideally, however, timber felling needs to be halted entirely to guarantee the long-term protection of a rainforest.

Practical measures

Recently, scientists have begun studying the forest canopy, using ropes and aerial walkways to take them high into the trees. Studying the life of the forest canopy will improve our overall knowledge of the rainforest ecosystem, but it does not help to stop the forests from being destroyed. In any case, some forests will have disappeared before the plants and animals they contain have been fully described by science.

Fortunately, the plight of the remaining rainforests has become the focus of international

concern in recent years. Conservation organizations like the International Union for the Conservation of Nature (IUCN), the World Wide Fund for Nature (WWF) and Friends of the Earth (FOE) have been successfully drawing people's attention to what is happening in the rainforests. Campaigns have also been mounted to try to protect specific areas, and also some of the most highly endangered rainforest animals, such as many species of primates.

Left A rainforest rally in Sydney, Australia. Northern Australia has its own extensive rainforests, some of them now under threat from cattle and sheep ranchers. Shown **below** *is Middle Gorge, Queensland.*

An Amazonian saman, or 'rain tree' in bloom. Its future survival depends on the successful conservation of the South American rainforests.

Regrowing a rainforest

In northern Costa Rica, South America, there is a special area of rainforest called dry forest. The trees that grow here are very rare and are now preserved in a small national park called Santa Rosa. An American botanist, Dr. Dan Janzen, would like to see them cover a much wider area, and has devised an ingenious way of doing this. His plan, which is being supported by the Costa Rican Government, the Worldwide Fund for Nature, and many local landowners, is as follows:

Cattle from nearby farmland are allowed to graze in the national park and wander back on to their farms. At the same time, local farmers are encouraged to let the wild animals of the national park (for example tapirs) roam on to their land. In this way, the seeds of the rare dry forest trees that the cattle and the wild animals have eaten are transported by the animals and passed out in their droppings on to the farmland. Eventually, it is hoped the seeds will become trees which the farmers can use selectively for fuel. There would still be enough room for grazing land between the new trees on the farmland areas.

It is planned that the existing national park and the new dry forest area will combine to form a much larger national park called Guanacaste. This is the name of a well-known species of dry forest tree that used to flourish all along the Pacific coast of Central America.

A project designed to conserve a rainforest normally has several different aims. Firstly, it must establish or strengthen protection for the area. This may involve persuading the government of the country to give it the status of a national park or reserve. It is also necessary to train people to act as guards or forest rangers, to protect the rainforest and its animals from poachers. Scientific surveys of the plants and animals will be required, to find out which are in most urgent need of protection. Finally, local peoples need to be made aware that the rainforest area is under protection. They should also be told the benefits of leaving it intact. Without their understanding and goodwill, the success of the venture is far less likely.

All of these factors require equipment, personnel and time, which in turn cost a great deal of money. Until recently, funds for conservation work came directly from public donations together with a proportion of money from the governments concerned. Recently however, a number of industrial companies, both large and small, have become involved in the crusade to save the disappearing rainforests. They are sponsoring projects which are carried out jointly with the conservation organizations.

The car company, Jaguar, is involved with the creation and maintenance of forest reserves in South America, which are the home of the large spotted cat which is the company's emblem. The forests of the Manu National Park in Peru and the Tortuguero National Park in Costa Rica have been further protected by grants from industry. Manu

---

Rainforest conservation projects sponsored by WWF and IUCN

Belize	Management of howler monkey sanctuary.	**India**	Management of the nine tiger forest reserves established since 1973.
Brazil	Project to improve rainforest conservation education.	**Indonesia**	Study of the medicinal use of plants in the forests of Siberut, near Sumatra.
Brazil	Reintroduction of golden lion tamarin. Management of reserves for endangered bird species.	**Madagascar**	Management of Beza-Mahalaly Forest Reserve. Training of local students.
Cameroon	Creation of Korup National Park.	**Malaysia**	Protection of Sumatran rhinoceros and orang-utan.
Chile	Collection and propagation programmes for rare rainforest plants.	**Peru**	Manu National Park created 1968 to protect jaguar, ocelot, giant otter and Brazilian tapir.
Colombia	Prevention of poaching in Cahuinari National Park.		
Ecuador	Management of coastal forest in Machalila National Park.	**Rwanda**	Prevention of gorilla poaching.

National Park actually contains 10 per cent of all bird species found in the world! In the Central American country of Belize, the giant multi-national Coca-Cola company has donated a large area of land for the creation of a new rainforest reserve. Perhaps some other companies will follow this example.

Across the other side of the Atlantic Ocean in central Africa, a number of other projects are under way. The Korup Forest of Cameroon was the subject of a television documentary. Now it has been turned into a national park and several European companies, including the Midland Bank are helping to meet the expenses of its upkeep. Korup is believed to contain the most

The jaguar is the largest predator in the rainforests of Central and South America. Hunted extensively in the past for their skins, these cats are now safe in reserves sponsored by the car manufacturer, Jaguar.

species of plants so far discovered in an African rainforest. Elsewhere in central Africa, industry is helping to finance studies of gorillas and chimpanzees in Gabon, and the conservation of the forest home of mountain gorillas, in Uganda. The Italian car-makers, Fiat, are sponsoring projects to protect the lemurs of Madagascar. This country's few remaining patches of rainforest are the only home of these remarkable primates.

Korup National Park, Cameroon

Korup contains a quarter of all Africa's primates, 250 species of birds and 400 species of trees. Many of Korup's animals, including elephants and leopards, are at risk from hunters, who earn a living from the skin trade. In March 1988 the Cameroon Government and WWF agreed on a plan to save the Korup rainforest, while at the same time providing income for the local people. Under the scheme a 'buffer zone' was created around the precious rainforest. Here the local people may grow crops and timber, manage fish farms and breed animals for hunting. This unique project may be a model for similar schemes in other countries.

Above *In the buffer zone around Korup, tree nurseries have been created to provide fast-growing timber for local people.*

Below *Korup is Africa's richest remaining rainforest.*

The forests of South-east Asia are equally important. Here, the British stationers, W H Smith, and the publishers, Batsford, are providing money to help conserve large mammals like tigers, rhinoceros and elephants which inhabit the rainforests of Indonesia. In southern China, a management plan is being developed to protect the rainforests in the Xishuangbanna Reserve.

Another by-product of the rainforest which, until recently, has been overlooked, is tourism. Now several countries are looking to tourism as a way of making their remaining forests pay. Successful tourism means the forests are saved from the axe or chainsaw, and their animal inhabitants safeguarded. However, tourism depends on people's willingness to travel long distances to see for themselves what a rainforest is like. Already in the central African countries of Rwanda and Zaire, the endangered mountain gorillas of the rainforests have successfully attracted tourists. In learning about the gorillas, visitors also learn about the forests as a whole. So tourism not only provides much-needed revenue, but also the chance to show people why forest conservation is vital.

These are just a few examples of the tremendous efforts now being made to protect our rainforests. For some areas help may already be too late. An example is the rainforest of Brazil, which contains some of the world's rarest primates. Elsewhere, it seems that we have a good chance to save some of the remaining rainforests. If we do succeed, we then have to make sure what is left of this unique environment is kept intact for the future. This is the only way to safeguard the magnificent array of plants and animals which live in rainforests.

Rwanda's mountain gorillas have become a popular tourist attraction, and a flourishing asset to the country's economy.

How can you help?

The current rate of rainforest destruction is alarming, and it is easy to feel depressed by it. However, as you have been reading, much work is being done to preserve rainforests and protect their unique wildlife.

You can play your part by finding out as much as possible about what is happening to rainforests. You can help by talking to your friends and relatives about rainforests, and telling them why they are so important to us.

Above all, you can help by joining an international conservation organization. Many of them are listed on page 47. By becoming a member, you will be supporting the funds of the organization, so helping them to do their valuable work in preserving rainforests for all of us.

'The loss of tropical rainforests is the most crucial ecological issue of our time.'

Catherine Caufield, Author of 'In the Rainforest'.

Glossary

Altitude   The height of a place above sea level.

Amphibious   Having the ability to live both on land and in the water, like frogs and newts.

Botanist   A person who studies plants.

Camouflaged   Coloured or shaped to blend in with the surroundings.

Deciduous   Plants whose leaves are shed once a year, normally at a particular time.

Decomposes   Rots down.

Dormant   In a state of deep sleep or inactivity.

Ecosystem   A community of plants and animals and the environment in which they live.

Equator   An imaginary line around the centre of the earth, between the North and South pole.

Erosion   The wearing down of land by the action of wind and water, which gradually remove the soil or rocks.

Evergreen   Plants with thick, waxy leaves which are not shed at regular intervals.

Fauna   All the animal life of a given place.

Flora   All the plant life of a given place.

Habitat   The natural home of particular plant and animal species.

Herbivorous   Feeding on plants.

Invertebrates   Animals without backbones.

Mammal   A warm-blooded animal with hair or fur on its body, whose young are fed on milk.

New World   The continent of America which was discovered after the Old World.

Nutrients   Organisms which provide nourishment for the growth of plants or animals.

Old World   That part of the world (Europe, Asia, and Africa) that was known before the discovery of the Americas.

Poaching   Illegally catching and killing animals for food and other products.

Pollute   To poison the land, water or air with chemical waste and factory smoke.

Predator   An animal which hunts another animal.

Prehensile   Having the ability to coil up the tail and use it as a fifth limb.

Primates   A type of mammal typically having flexible hands and feet with opposable first digits. Monkeys, apes and humans are primates.

Species   A group of animals or plants, different from all other groups, that can breed together to produce young, which can also breed together.

Sponsor   A person or company that gives money to support an organization.

Tropics   The area of the world situated between the Tropic of Cancer and the Tropic of Capricorn.

Vegetation.   All the different species of plants, including trees, which grow together in one area.

Picture acknowledgements

The photographs in this book are by: Ardea London Ltd 4, 6; David Bowden/WPL 40; Bruce Coleman Ltd *Cover* (Gerald Cubitt), 5, 7, 8, 16 left, 17, 19 above, 21, 22 above and below, 24 below, 28 main picture, 29, 31, 32 above and below, 34, 35, 36, 38, 39, 45; ICCE 41 below, 44 below; Frank Lane 16 right; Oxford Scientific Films 13, 14, 15, 18, 19 below, 20 above, 23, 33 above and below, 37, 40 below, 44 below; Tony Morrison 10, 13 below, 15 above, 20 below, 24 above, 27, 28 inset, 30, 43; WWF/UK 44 above. The illustrations are by Brian Watson.

Further reading

Attenborough, D. *The Living Planet* (Collins 1984).
Banks, M. *Endangered Wildlife* (Wayland 1987).
Caufield, C. *In the Rainforest* (Heinemann 1985).
Flenly, J. *The Equatorial Rainforest. A geological history* (Butterworth 1979).
King, P. *Protect our Planet* (Quiller Press 1986).
Markham, A. *The Environment* (Wayland 1988).
Mitchell, A. *The Enchanted Canopy* (Collins 1986).

Pye-Smith, C. *World Conservation* (Macdonald 1984).
Richards, P. *The Tropical Rainforest* (Cambridge University Press 1981).
Rowland-Entwistle, T. *Jungles and Rainforests* (Wayland 1987).
Taylor, N. *Plant drugs that changed the world* (Allen and Unwin 1966).

Magazines

BBC Wildlife (monthly)
Oryx (Journal of the Fauna and Flora Preservation Society)

There are also many superb television documentaries about rainforests and their fascinating wildlife.

Useful addresses

Friends of the Earth
377 City Road
London EC1

Greenpeace (UK)
30-31 Islington Green
London N1 8XE

Greenpeace (USA)
1611 Connecticut Avenue N.W.
Washington DC2009

Greenpeace (Australia)
310 Angas Street
Adelaide 5000

Greenpeace (Canada)
2623 West 4th Avenue
Vancouver BCV6K 1P8

World Wide Fund for Nature
Panda House
Weyside Park
Godalming Surrey

Places to visit

Zoos
Most zoos have some rainforest animals, including lemurs and monkeys and wild cats. Some zoos have breeding programmes for rare rainforest animals.

Tropical bird gardens
Here you can see brightly-coloured rainforest birds, such as parrots and toucans. Some gardens have special tropical houses where humming-birds fly freely.

Butterfly farms
Most of these have heated glass houses where you can see beautiful tropical butterflies flying freely.

Botanical gardens
Many gardens contain hot houses where rainforest plants and trees can grow. Two excellent examples are Missouri, USA and Kew Gardens, London.

Index